D0062584

"Since Caleb is one of my greatest heroes, I plunged into *The Caleb Quest* with real interest. I was rewarded! Mark offers gracious encouragement, vital warnings, and a clear roadmap to safeguard the unique dream that God plants within each of our hearts."

—STEVE GREEN
RECORDING ARTIST

"Most of us spend a lifetime chasing our dreams. *The Caleb Quest* offers direction, perspective, and guidance in bringing these dreams to reality. A real winner!"

—LEEMAN BENNETT
TWO-TIME NFL COACH OF THE YEAR

"The cornerstone of dynamic spiritual leadership in the home, church, or community is the dream . . . that is, a vision or a strong sense of how God is at work in you and how he is going to work through you in the lives of others. *The Caleb Quest* is a thorough, fresh, and compelling look at the man whom Mark Atteberry calls 'the boldest dreamer in the Bible.' Since I know Mark to be an exceptional preacher, I was not surprised to discover that his writing is equally engaging. I cannot imagine a better handbook for use in both determining and achieving a God-honored dream."

—KEN IDLEMAN
PRESIDENT, OZARK CHRISTIAN COLLEGE
JOPLIN, MO

"Pastor Mark, once again you have uncovered truth and treasure from a mostly untapped resource in the Bible. *The Caleb Quest* has refortified my position that the dreams God puts in our hearts do come true if we are willing to become active dreamers."

—Dr. Ben Lerner

America's Maximized-Living Mentor
Author of the *New York Times* bestseller
Body by God

"Tell it like it is, Mark! *The Caleb Quest* didn't motivate me to dream something unattainable. Instead, it gave me biblical guidelines to see if my dreams line up with God's plan. I'm much wiser after this big dose of reality! Eye-opening and refreshing!"

—Melissa Montana

General Manager of STAR 88.3
Host of daily radio show "Conversations"

THE
CALEB
QUEST

WHAT YOU CAN
LEARN FROM THE
BOLDEST DREAMER
IN THE BIBLE

MARK ATTEBERRY

THOMAS NELSON
Since 1798

NASHVILLE   DALLAS   MEXICO CITY   RIO DE JANEIRO   BEIJING

© 2004 by Mark Atteberry

All rights reserved. No portion of this book may be reproduced, stored in a retrieval system, or transmitted in any form or by any means—electronic, mechanical, photocopy, recording, scanning, or other—except for brief quotations in critical reviews or articles, without the prior written permission of the publisher.

Published in Nashville, Tennessee, by Thomas Nelson. Thomas Nelson is a registered trademark of Thomas Nelson, Inc.

Thomas Nelson, Inc., titles may be purchased in bulk for educational, business, fund-raising, or sales promotional use. For information, please e-mail SpecialMarkets@ThomasNelson.com.

Author is represented by the literary agency of Alive Communications, Inc., 7680 Goddard Street, Suite 200, Colorado Springs, CO 80920.

Scripture quotations are taken from the *Holy Bible,* New Living Translation, copyright © 1996. Used by permission of Tyndale House Publishers, Inc., Wheaton, Illinois 60189. All rights reserved.

Library of Congress Cataloging-in-Publication Data

Atteberry, Mark.
  The Caleb quest : what you can learn from the boldest dreamer in the Bible / Mark Atteberry.
    p. cm.
  ISBN 978-0-7852-6187-2 (hardcover)
  ISBN 978-0-7852-8784-1 (tradepaper)
  1. Success—Religious aspects—Christianity. 2. Caleb (Biblical figure)
I. Title.
  BV4598.3.A75 2004
  248.4—dc22   2004001711

Printed in the United States of America
09 10 11 12 LSI 6 5 4 3 2 1

FOR MY WIFE, MARILYN.

YOU ARE MY ULTIMATE DREAM COME TRUE.

CONTENTS

FOREWORD

WE ARE ALL BORN WITH A DESIRE DEEP WITHIN us. A seed, a dream, a promise of something greater.

You've felt it, haven't you? That certain knowing that somehow, somewhere, a destiny lives in your soul, one that will rise up every now and then and tap you on the shoulder with a reminder of that special thing you were created to be.

Or maybe you've felt it and figured it wasn't for you, not really a calling after all. Maybe you've given up on that lifelong dream. If so, the treasures that lie in the pages of this book will change your mind. About dreams and purpose, and especially about giving up.

The Bible has a story about a man named Caleb, who understood that feeling, that thing that we sometimes spend a lifetime chasing. And so Mark Atteberry brings you his eye-opening, heart-grabbing book: *The Caleb Quest*.

Maybe what I love most about Mark's book is that he gets it. He understands the Caleb Quest idea, because deep within his heart he has harbored a dream bigger than the sun. And he, knowing this, prayed and begged and searched God on the matter until finally, in all of heaven's splendor, events and times and souls came together and Mark saw his dream through to completion.

And all of us who knew Mark could almost see God smiling.

If you've never taken the time in your busy, scheduled, automated world to think about that which grows inside you, sit back and relax. Your time has come. As you read *The Caleb Quest,* you cannot help but hear God's voice reminding you of this: you have a purpose, a passion inside you. You know, the one that makes you wonder whether to become a teacher, a doctor, a missionary.

Or even a writer.

Read on, and let the dreams within you breathe and grow. Dust off the doubts and run with abandon into the future God has placed in your heart.

You see, God made us in His image, and that's what *The Caleb Quest* is all about, really: a God-sized dream, living and growing way down inside us, causing a desire so strong it can only be satisfied by our heeding it—heeding it and giving everything we have to making it come true.

Perhaps it's this part of us, this quest within us, that makes us most like God. After all, Jesus' entire life was one world-rocking, gate-opening, devil-thumping quest. Jesus was born with the single dream of seeing the world saved, seeing heaven's gates flung wide open for those who believe. It was a quest He pursued with every step, every word, every breath.

Right up until the end.

Christ's ultimate quest led Him to the cross. But even as He hung there, flesh ripped open, spat upon, mocked, and dying, the dream was in sight. Pursuing His life's passion culminated in a trip to Golgotha, a journey that seemed to those present nothing more than bitter defeat. Ah, but even then Christ rejoiced.

For all the power of hell couldn't change the fact that as His personal quest was coming to an end, Jesus could see the light.

"It is finished," He said as He died. And with that, death was destroyed, His quest completed.

Even though it cost our God everything He had to give.

Remember that the next time you think about giving up.

KAREN KINGSBURY

PREFACE

I WROTE THIS LITTLE BOOK IN RESPONSE TO some questions that had been troubling me for quite a few years. As a pastor, I know all too well that countless Christians are discouraged by the course their lives have taken. Many good, well-intentioned people started out years ago with ambitious dreams and enough energy and determination to make them come true ten times over. But today they are looking back and wondering what went wrong. Their dreams have fizzled, and, in some cases, turned to nightmares. The dream job was never offered, the dream marriage lost its fire, the dream kids went astray, and the dream house was never built.

All of this seems quite odd when you stop to consider that our Lord promised the fulfillment of our dreams. He said, "You can ask for anything in my name, and I will do it, because the work of the Son brings glory to the Father. Yes, ask anything in my name and I will do it!" (John 14:13–14). He also said, "Keep on asking, and you will be given what you ask for. Keep on looking, and you will find. Keep on knocking, and the door will be opened. For everyone who asks, receives. Everyone who seeks, finds. And the door is opened to everyone who knocks" (Luke 11:9–10).

If these promises are true, then why are so many of God's people mourning the death of their dreams?

Has God been unfaithful to His promises?

Do dreams really come true?

And if so, what does it take to make them happen?

These are the questions that troubled me.

I now believe God has answered these questions in the life of Caleb, the boldest dreamer and achiever in all of God's Word. I'm convinced that the main reason his story was included in Scripture is to show us that dreams really do come true, not just in Disney movies, but in real life.

This book follows Caleb's quest to conquer the hill country of Hebron, from his initial spy mission behind enemy lines to his final victory more than forty years later. The foundational truth of this book is that there's a lot involved in making a dream come true. With all due respect to that famous insect philosopher, Jiminy Cricket, merely wishing upon a star doesn't cut it. Caleb shows us that fulfilled dreams are the result of clear thinking, strong faith, patience, and lots of hard work. So be forewarned: the Caleb Quest is no pie-in-the-sky prescription for wealth and happiness. It rejects the "name it and claim it" theology that has left so many confused and discouraged. Instead, it offers a down-to-earth, biblical, workable plan for making your lifelong dream come true.

At this moment, you could well be at a God-ordained crossroads in your life. After years of disappointment, you could finally be holding in your hands the answers you've been looking for. You could be just on the verge of discovering why things haven't worked out for you in the past. And you could be only a few pages away from finally understanding how to get from where you are to where you've always wanted to be.

Imagine.

Hope could be resurrected in your heart.

Your faith in God could be renewed.

Suddenly, your life could have meaning and purpose again.

If you're one of the countless people who've never had a dream come true, or if you're carrying a great dream in your heart but don't know how to start pursuing it, I hope you'll turn the page, not just in this book, but in your life. I hope you'll open your mind to some fresh ideas and give yourself a chance to go where you've never been, to see what you've never seen, and to experience what you've never experienced.

I hope you'll join the Caleb Quest.

ONE

ASSESSING YOUR DREAM

You see things and you say, "Why?"
But I see things that never were, and say, "Why not?"
—GEORGE BERNARD SHAW

I PICTURE THE MEN ASSEMBLING LATE ONE evening, emerging from the shadows to gather around a crackling campfire. They probably didn't know why they had been called, and some of them may well have felt irritated at the interruption of their evening's activities. But the summons had come from Moses himself, and that was enough to set them in motion. From all

1

corners of the camp they came, twelve men in all, one from each tribe, the brightest and the best.

I can imagine Moses greeting the men one by one, renewing acquaintances and asking about wives and children. Perhaps the men were also greeting one another and whispering among themselves, speculating as to the reason why they were called. I'm sure they didn't have to wait long to find out. Having made the rounds, I picture Moses stepping toward the fire and asking the men to be seated. He probably thanked them for coming and then told them, without any hesitation, that he was calling upon them to undertake an important mission.

They would be sent as a team across the Jordan River and into the land of Canaan. Their job would be to spy out the land that God had promised to give the nation of Israel. As discreetly as possible, they would head northward into the hill country and evaluate the enemy cities, their fortifications, and the quality of the land itself. They were also instructed to bring back samples of the fruits and vegetables so the people of Israel could see for themselves that it was a bountiful land, one that would meet all of their needs when the time came to move in.

As Moses laid out the plan, I'm sure excitement

passed through the group like an electric current. The sense of adventure that resides in such men needs only a nudge to set it spinning. If the customs of our day had been in vogue at that time, they probably would have been congratulating each other with high fives and pumping fists. I wouldn't be surprised if Moses had to temper their enthusiasm with a solemn reminder that it would be a dangerous campaign, lasting many weeks.

I picture the men dispersing quickly after the briefing. No doubt they were anxious to share the news with their wives and to think and pray about what lay ahead. Because they had lived for so many years as slaves in Egypt, none of them were experienced soldiers. Oh yes, they were plenty tough and capable. Hard labor and the crack of a whip across your back will make you as tough as a two-dollar steak. But none of them had any experience in clandestine operations. My guess is that, in spite of their outward expressions of machismo, they all did some tossing and turning that night, wondering how the mission would unfold and how it might change them.

Looking back, it's clear that one of those men was changed more than any other. His name was Caleb, the son of Jephunneh. What happened to him during those forty days of undercover work is something that happens to almost everybody, sooner or later: he found his lifelong dream.

What's odd is that he apparently wasn't looking for it. Over the years I've often heard it said that young people in particular ought to look for a dream. Books have even been written about how to find your heart's desire. But when Caleb stepped out of the Jordan River onto Canaan's fertile soil, there's no indication that he had anything on his mind other than fulfilling his mission.

Oh, how quickly and how dramatically our lives can change!

The moment he set his eyes on the hill country of Hebron, his heart began to pound like a hammer in his chest. He'd never seen a more beautiful place. And though it was inhabited by a race of giants, he began to imagine living and raising his family in those beautiful hills. The mere idea thrilled his soul and painted a thousand pictures on the canvas of his mind. And every one was a masterpiece.

> THE BEST DREAM IS THE ONE THAT FINDS YOU, RATHER THAN THE ONE YOU HAVE TO FIND.

4

As I've studied Caleb's story, I've come to the conclusion that the best dream is the one that finds you, rather than the one you have to find. I wouldn't dare suggest that a dreamless person shouldn't go looking for one. Perhaps many great achievers had to search for their dreams for many years. But when you are blindsided . . . when the vision of something you'd like to be or do knocks you off your feet, you have every reason to believe it will become the great, driving passion of your life. And it's those great, driving passions that stand the best chance of coming true.

If you're a lover of the ocean, you're probably familiar with an artist named Wyland. He is the world's foremost painter of ocean art and is even listed in the *Guinness Book of World Records* for having painted the world's largest mural. It's a breathtaking ocean scene on the front of the Long Beach Convention Center that is—are you ready for this?—one-fifth of a mile long!

What's interesting is that Wyland was born with a clubfoot and endured eleven surgeries before his seventh birthday. Because he was unable to run and play with his friends and siblings, he often sat in the house and drew pictures. He demonstrated a special talent for art, but he never thought it would become his life's work.

Until one day when he had a head-on collision with his dream.

In 1971 he was visiting relatives in Laguna Beach, California. His aunt drove him to the beach and he sat there, staring out over the water. Suddenly and unexpectedly, two enormous whales broke the surface in a majestic display of power and grace. To this day, Wyland says that moment was a turning point in his life. Something about the sheer beauty of that scene made him want to use his artistic talent to help people understand and appreciate the wonders of the sea. He reasoned that if people came to love it, they would want to protect it.

As of this writing, Wyland has painted more than eighty public murals, which he calls *Whaling Walls.* These murals represent more than 64 million square feet of art, for which he has cheerfully donated his labor and at least eighty thousand gallons of paint. In addition, there are almost a quarter of a million Wyland collectors in seventy countries. Oh yes, and did I mention that he has also written five books and is working on a science curriculum with the Scripps Oceanographic Institute that will impact millions of school kids?[1]

Every time my wife, Marilyn, and I visit the Wyland Gallery near our home, we are reminded of what can happen when a man and a dream collide.

Right now, do you have a dream?

I'm not just talking about something you're *hoping* for, but something you're *living* for. Something you think about every day. Something that quickens your pulse when it crosses your mind. Something that affects the decisions you make. Something you'd even be willing to risk your life for, if it came to that.

Do you have *that* kind of dream?

If so, then I'm glad God saw fit to place this book in your hands. Of all the people a passionate dreamer needs to get to know, Caleb is at the top of the list because he was a man who actually fulfilled his lifelong dream. It wasn't easy, as we will see. But he did it, and by taking a close look at his story, you and I can learn how to do it too.

The place to start is with the dream itself.

It's safe to say that there are good dreams and bad

dreams. Dreams that are worthy of our time and effort, and dreams that are not. Dreams that will mold and shape us into better people, and dreams that will tear us down. Dreams that will draw us closer to God, and dreams that will carry us away from Him. A close look at Caleb's dream will reveal three reasons why it was a good one and, at the same time, give us the tools we need to assess our own.

CALEB'S DREAM FIT WITH GOD'S WILL

From the very beginning, God made it clear that He wanted His people to inhabit the land of Canaan. Hundreds of years before Caleb was born, Abram and his family left Haran and entered the territory for the first time. Near a place called Shechem, the Lord appeared to him and said, "I am going to give this land to your offspring" (Gen. 12:7). Caleb would have been well aware of that promise, which is, no doubt, the primary reason he held onto his dream for so many years with such unwavering confidence. It makes a world of difference when you know beyond any doubt that God is on your side!

Right now, it's important that you take a look at your dream in the light of what God has said. It doesn't matter how passionate you are about it or how relentlessly you're willing to pursue it. If God doesn't approve of your dream, then it's in serious trouble. Check out these powerful verses: "Everything in the heavens and on earth is yours, O LORD . . . Riches and honor come from you alone, for you rule over everything. Power and might are in your hand, and *it is at your discretion that people are made great and given strength*" (1 Chron. 29:11–12, italics mine).

Read that last part again slowly, and let it sink in.

God is ultimately the one who determines who among us achieves greatness and receives strength. We often talk about successful people being lucky or in the right place at the right time, but clearly there's more to it than that. God is constantly helping some people and hindering others.

> IT DOESN'T MATTER HOW PASSIONATE YOU ARE ABOUT IT OR HOW RELENTLESSLY YOU'RE WILLING TO PURSUE IT. IF GOD DOESN'T APPROVE OF YOUR DREAM, THEN IT'S IN SERIOUS TROUBLE.

9

Do I understand all of His choices? Can I always explain why Person A gets His blessing and Person B doesn't? Absolutely not. His thoughts are much too deep for me. But I know this much: when it comes to *my* dream, I want His approval, not His disapproval. I want His favor, not His opposition. Therefore, I am going to do everything in my power to make sure my dream fits with His will. I want Him to look at me and say, "Yes, My son, I like what you have in mind."

I've often found it beneficial to take verses of Scripture and frame them in opposite terms. It's kind of like shining a spotlight on an object from the opposite direction. The object itself is unchanged, but you can discover features that you never noticed before. Take Romans 8:31, for example. Paul asked, "If God is for us, who can ever be against us?" That's a verse we love to quote because it makes us feel warm and fuzzy. But look what happens when you frame the question in opposite terms: "If God is *against* us, what difference does it make who's *for* us?" Packs a punch, doesn't it?

Listen, my dreaming friend, you simply must take a hard look at your dream and make sure it fits with God's will. Don't be afraid. Some people assume that

God's will is a tiny island in an endless ocean of aspirations, but nothing could be further from the truth. God's will is, in fact, a vast territory that allows for a wide array of goals and desires.

So get out your Bible and see if your dream is compatible with what God has said. If it isn't, you're on your own. You have no reason to think you'll get any help from God. And without some help from the one who "rules over everything," what hope do you have of succeeding? In all honesty, you might as well close this book right now and go on about your business. Nothing you will read from here on will help you if you've already committed to a course of action that puts you in opposition to God.

On the other hand, if you've searched the Scriptures and know that your dream fits with God's will, then read on. You've already taken the first and most important step in the right direction.

CALEB'S DREAM FIT WITH HIS TALENTS

Have you ever wondered why Joshua succeeded Moses as the leader of Israel, when Caleb was just as faithful and committed? The reason undoubtedly had to do with their gifts. Deuteronomy 34:9 indicates that a special bond existed between Moses and Joshua, probably because Joshua was a natural-born student who loved to sit and learn at Moses' feet. They probably spent countless hours together, much of it one-on-one, as Joshua soaked up his mentor's accumulated wisdom.

Caleb, on the other hand, was more a man of action, as indicated by the fact that his motor was still running at the age of eighty-five (Josh. 14:10–11). He probably found it difficult to sit still long enough to be trained in the subtleties of diplomacy and political gamesmanship. He was the guy you called when you had a job that needed doing!

And so, Caleb's dream fit with his talents. Taking the hill country of Hebron was not something Israel could accomplish through diplomatic channels. It was going to be achieved on the battlefield, under the leadership of someone strong and courageous. Thus, it was the perfect dream for a doer like Caleb.

Have you ever evaluated your dream in the light of your talents?

Several years ago, a Major League Baseball team held

a tryout near our home. It was open to the public, so I decided to stop by and check it out. About forty young men between the ages of eighteen and twenty-four had assembled with their cleats and gloves, determined to prove that they had big-league potential. For about an hour and a half, coaches put them through a series of hitting and fielding drills and timed them in the forty-yard dash. At the end of the day, not one of the young men was offered a contract.

To be honest, even my untrained eye could see that there wasn't a big-leaguer in the bunch. Several of them were overweight and slow, and one poor fellow took at least a dozen swings in the cage and never even hit a foul ball! Some of the guys were so pathetic, I actually found myself feeling sorry for them.

I don't want to rain on your parade, but before we get too far into this study, you might as well face up to the fact that there are some things in life you will *never* be able to do.

If you're tone-deaf, you'll never be an opera singer. (Rap, maybe, but not opera!)

If you have two left feet, you'll never be an Olympic gymnast.

If you can't stand the sight of blood, you'll never make it as a surgeon.

If you're six-foot-six and weigh 350 pounds, you have no future as a jockey.

Mark this down: God's blessings are always going to harmonize with His gifts.

Read that again slowly and let it soak in because it's one of the most important truths in this book.

God's blessings are *always* going to harmonize with His gifts.

In other words, He's not going to bless your efforts to achieve something that He hasn't gifted you to do. Romans 12:6 says, "God has given each of us the ability to do *certain things* well" (italics mine). You can be sure that it will be in those "certain things" that you'll find His blessing.

And while we're on the subject of talents, let me mention one more thing.

I've heard it said that the secret of success is hard work; that you can be a success at anything if you're willing to work hard enough. While I agree that dreams don't come true without a lot of effort, I also believe that no amount of hard work will overcome a lack of talent. In other words, all the singing lessons in the world won't help you if you're tone-deaf.

So why take those lessons?

Samuel Johnson said, "Almost every man wastes part of his life trying to display qualities which he does not possess."

Wouldn't it make more sense to invest that time and energy in some talent you *do* possess? It sounds noble to say that you're going to work on your weaknesses, but wouldn't it benefit you more to work on your strengths? Then, instead of just being good at something, you could become great. Instead of just being one of the many, you could become one of the few. By working hard and reaching your highest potential in the area of your giftedness, you will move yourself ahead of all the people who may be equally talented but not as committed. And in a highly competitive

BY WORKING HARD AND REACHING YOUR HIGHEST POTENTIAL IN THE AREA OF YOUR GIFTEDNESS, YOU WILL MOVE YOURSELF AHEAD OF ALL THE PEOPLE WHO MAY BE EQUALLY TALENTED BUT NOT AS COMMITTED.

15

world, that's an essential part of making your dream come true.

CALEB'S DREAM FIT WITH ISRAEL'S NEED

One of the first things you realize about Caleb's dream is that it was going to benefit the entire nation. Clearing the race of giants known as Anakim out of the hill country was something Israel would have to do, sooner or later, if the people were going to enjoy any degree of peace in their new homeland. That Caleb was itching to do the job was an unexpected and very welcome blessing for everyone.

Have you thought about how your dream would impact the people around you if it were to come true?

When I was a kid, I dreamed of being a professional jazz musician. I lived in a home where jazz was played almost constantly, and my dad, who owned thousands of jazz records, took my brother and me to see all the big bands when they passed through our neck of the woods. At the same time, I was playing saxophone in the school band and getting in trouble almost daily for improvising when I was supposed to be sticking to the printed music. By the time I was sixteen, I couldn't imagine doing anything else with my life.

But all of that changed one night in Evansville, Indiana.

As the result of a summer music camp, my family had become acquainted with a jazz saxophonist who was touring the country with the Stan Kenton Orchestra. One night before a concert at Vanderburgh Auditorium, we picked him up and took him to dinner. I was in awe. I remember hanging on every word as he told fascinating stories about life in the jazz world.

And then something happened that turned out to be a dagger in my dream.

He had ordered a 7-Up, and after sipping about a third of it, he stood up, excused himself, and carried his glass to the restroom. I thought that was the strangest thing I had ever seen and made a comment to that effect. Who ever heard of taking your drink to the restroom? That's when my dad quietly explained what was happening.

Sure enough, when he returned to the table, the glass was full and a slightly different color. He'd topped it off with liquor from a flask in his pocket. My dad had known it all along, but at my age and in my state of blind euphoria, I'd missed the signs.

The man was a hard-core alcoholic.

That night, on the way home, my dad talked to me about the many temptations that professional musicians face and how some are swallowed up by them. He said, "If you want to be a musician, that's fine. But just understand that it'll be hard on you as a Christian, and if you have a family, it'll be hard on them too."

I can't say that I abandoned my dream that day, but I can say that it never quite looked the same to me again. And as I got older and became a little wiser, I saw even more clearly that the things professional traveling musicians have to contend with, such as worldly environments and long periods of separation from their families, could mean trouble for someone like me. And not just for me, but for the people I loved.

> WE HAVE A WORD FOR HOLLOW DREAMS THAT COME TRUE. THEY'RE CALLED NIGHTMARES.

As you assess your dream, it's important for you to think beyond yourself. Philippians 2:4 says, "Don't think only about your own affairs, but be interested in others, too." Your dream may be something you think you can't live without. But if it isn't good for the people God has placed in your sphere of influence, then it isn't good, period.

, , ,

I realize that, at this point, you might be feeling quite discouraged. If you've dissected your dream and found that it doesn't fit with God's will, your talents, or the needs of the people around you, you now face the prospect of discarding it. That can be hard, especially if it's a dream you've been carrying in your heart for a long time.

But look at it another way.

Now is the best time to make that discovery, not after the dream has come true. Imagine how sick you'd be if you spent your entire life chasing a dream and finally achieved it only to discover that it was hollow all along. Keep this in mind: we have a word for hollow dreams that come true. They're called nightmares.

Believe me, there is a *good* dream out there some-where with your name on it. Maybe it hasn't found you yet (or you haven't found it), but remember this: on the night that Moses called the twelve spies together, Caleb hadn't yet connected with his lifelong dream. However, it was just over the horizon. He didn't know it, but he was relentlessly marching toward it. Maybe you are too. Maybe today will be the day when your lifelong dream will strike like a bolt out of the blue and knock you off your feet. Or maybe it will happen tomorrow. The important thing is to believe it's out there.

On the other hand, maybe you're coming to the end of this chapter with a sense of excitement, because your dream *has* passed the test. If so, you're ready to read on. Chapter 2 will focus on a sobering but important truth you simply must face: all truly great dreams have deadly enemies.

TWO

DREAM KILLERS

We grew up believing in Cinderella, yet some of us feel our palace turned out to be a duplex, our prince turned out to be a frog, and the wicked stepmother turned out to be our mother-in-law.

—BETH MOORE

WHEN YOUR DREAM HAS ALL THE GOOD THINGS going for it that we just considered in chapter 1, you can be sure that Satan will try to kill it. He knows that killing your dream will strike a blow against God's will. It will deprive you of the joy that only a dream come true can bring. And it will rob the people around you of a blessing. Every dead dream means misery in the hearts of men, and that's why Satan takes dream killing so seriously.

You can be sure that, even as you read these words, assassins are stalking your dream. Let me mention three notorious dream killers that you should be prepared to face.

YOUR ENEMIES

When Caleb first laid his eyes on the hill country of Hebron, he saw more than just a beautiful, bountiful land. He also saw the sons of Anak. They were a race of giants that inhabited large, fortified cities. To understand how scary they must have looked, think about Goliath, who may have been one of their descendants. All by himself, that nine-foot-tall monster of a man managed to terrify and intimidate the entire army of Israel (1 Sam. 17:24). Imagine how frightening several entire cities filled with such giants must have looked!

Figuratively speaking, every great dreamer will encounter the sons of Anak. They are the people who stand between you and your dream: your sworn enemies, who will stop at nothing to see you fail.

On January 6, 1994, figure skater Nancy Kerrigan met her "sons of Anak" face to face. She was practicing at Cobo Arena in Detroit for the U.S. Olympic trials. Moments after she left the ice, an assailant ran toward her and swung a blunt object, which connected squarely with her right knee. She collapsed in pain while her attacker ran down a hallway, smashed his way through a Plexiglas door, and jumped into a waiting car. It turned out that Kerrigan was the victim of a conspiracy that one of her competitors, Tonya Harding, orchestrated. According to sworn testimony from Harding's husband, Jeff Gillooly, his wife approved the attack because she didn't think she could beat Kerrigan.

Though physical attacks like that one are not unheard of, most of the blows we'll face from our "sons of Anak" will be of the verbal variety. But that doesn't mean they'll be any less painful. An unjust criticism or a vicious rumor can be agonizing and take even longer to heal than a physical wound.

Caleb's story reveals two things that will help you defeat the enemies of your dream. They are *courage* and *trust in the Lord.* When the terrified people of Israel expressed a desire to turn away from the land of Canaan,

Caleb stood before them and said, "Let's go at once to take the land. We can certainly conquer it!" (Num. 13:30).

That's courage.

And then he and Joshua pleaded further, "Don't be afraid of the people of the land. They are only helpless prey to us! They have no protection, *but the LORD is with us!* Don't be afraid of them" (Num. 14:9, italics mine).

THE ENEMIES WHO COME AGAINST YOUR DREAM MIGHT BE STRONG—EVEN SCARY. BUT NO ENEMY CAN STAND AGAINST THE POWER AND THE PROVISIONS OF GOD.

That's trust.

Had the people heeded Caleb and Joshua's words, they could have marched into the land and taken it without a single casualty. God was all set to deliver on the promise He had made to Abraham many years before, and you can be sure He would have done it in spectacular fashion. Israel would have trampled the sons of Anak underfoot. Courage and trust would have saved the day.

That's something you need to remember when your "sons of Anak" appear on the horizon. Rest assured that if your dream is a good dream—one that fits with God's will, your talents, and the needs of the people around you—you don't have to be afraid to move forward. Paul said, "If God is for us, who can ever be against us?" (Rom. 8:31). And Jesus said that God "will give you all you need from day to day if you live for him" (Matt. 6:33).

I won't kid you; the enemies who come against your dream might be strong—even scary. But no enemy can stand against the power and the provisions of God.

YOUR FRIENDS

Have you ever been crabbing? (If fishing is what we're doing when we try to catch fish, I assume we're "crabbing" when we try to catch crabs.) You would think that catching crabs would be very difficult. After all, the little guys are quite agile, with all those legs sticking out in every direction. But they are actually quite easy to capture, and the reason is that they are natural-born dream killers.

Let me explain.

You don't catch crabs with hooks or nets. Instead, you use traps. A crab trap is nothing more than a wire basket with a hole in the top. The crabber puts some bait in the basket and lowers it into the water. Soon a crab comes along, walks into the basket, and starts chowing down. Then another crab shows up, and another, and another, and another, until the bottom of the basket has become a swarming tangle of antennae, legs, and pinchers.

Obviously, the bait doesn't last long in such a party atmosphere, but the crabber above doesn't worry. He knows that even when there's no longer a reason to stay in the basket, not a single crab will leave. Oh, a few might try, but they will be unsuccessful. You see, the crabber knows that if a crab starts to crawl out of the basket, the others will grab him and pull him back. If he tries to crawl out again, they will do the same thing. Eventually, if he simply refuses to take the hint, they will resort to violence. They'll rip off his claws. And if that *still* doesn't do the trick, they'll kill him.

Perhaps you've noticed that people can, at times, be pretty crabby. G. K. Chesterton nailed it when he said, "The Bible tells us to love our neighbors, and also our enemies; probably because they are generally the same people."

Caleb certainly found this to be true. The sons of

Anak, as imposing as they looked, were not nearly as threatening to his dream as his own crabby friends and relatives. His very own countrymen were so afraid of moving forward that they wanted to overthrow Moses and choose a new leader to take them back to Egypt (Num. 14:3–4). And when Caleb and Joshua refused to keep quiet about moving ahead into the land of Canaan, the people started plotting to stone them to death (Num. 14:10)!

My dreaming friend, I'm going to be as blunt as I can on this point, because it's absolutely critical. You simply must beware of your family and friends. I know that statement has an odd ring to it. We like to believe that our

WE LIKE TO BELIEVE THAT OUR LOVED ONES WILL ALWAYS BE OUR BIGGEST SUPPORTERS. BUT WE CAN'T ALWAYS COUNT ON IT.

loved ones will always be our biggest supporters. But we can't always count on it. If you ever try to climb out of the trap of conformity and separate yourself from the crowd, it's very likely that one of them (or maybe several) will try to grab you by the ankle and drag you back into the basket.

In fairness, all "crabby" friends and relatives are not created equal. There will be two types of dream killers among them.

First, there will be those whose motives are pure. They're not bad; they're just timid and afraid. They like to play it safe, and they think you should too. If they see you getting ready to step out on faith and do something risky in pursuit of your dream, they'll speak up and try to talk some sense into you. They'll point out all the terrible things that could happen. They'll even tell you stories about other people they've known who did the same thing and suffered terrible consequences.

These are obviously people who love you very much and don't want to see you get hurt. They think they're doing you a favor by enumerating the dangers you're facing. But even if their motives are pure and even if there's an element of truth to what they're saying, their words can be deadly to your dream.

Second, there are those whose motives are impure. This group is different from the first in one important way.

The first group is afraid you'll *fail* and is trying to stop you.

28

The second group is afraid you'll *succeed* and is trying to stop you.

They're often motivated by envy, jealousy, or a twisted sense of competition. They can be family members, teammates, coworkers, or even fellow church members, and because of their impure motives, they will often resort to unethical tactics in their efforts to slow you down. The poster boy for this type of dream killer would be Judas, one of the original twelve disciples, who tried to kill all of Jesus' dreams by betraying Him into the hands of the Jewish leaders.

Over the years, I've watched Satan do some of his best work through the families and friends of honest dreamers. Part of the problem is that the dreamer is often reluctant to take a firm stand against negative friends or family members. Just to keep the peace, he'll allow them to pound on his dreams in ways that he would never tolerate from his enemies.

If your dream is to have any chance of coming true, you simply must deal with those negative influences. Remember when Peter took a negative view of our Lord's prophecy that He would be crucified and raised on the third day? He said, "Heaven forbid, Lord!" And

Jesus responded with a stinging rebuke: "Get away from me, Satan! You are a dangerous trap to me. You are seeing things merely from a human point of view, and not from God's" (Matt. 16:22–23). Jesus loved Peter with all His heart, but He wasn't going to tolerate his negative thinking.

Now, I don't recommend that you stand up to your mother, your spouse, or your best friend and shout, "Get away from me, Satan!" That will just get you a one-way ticket to the doghouse. But you may indeed need to speak up in a nice way and defend your dream.

I remember reading that when Walt Disney was a young schoolboy, his teacher saw him drawing pictures of flowers. She said, "They're very nice, Walter, but you know, flowers don't have faces." He looked up and said, "Mine do."

I love that!

Even as a small boy, he had the gumption to stick up for his dreams and not let other people trample on them, which is, no doubt, one of the major reasons why he was so successful. (By the way, in Disney's classic animated feature, *Alice in Wonderland*, the flowers all had faces . . . and voices.)

The bottom line is, you must find a way to insulate yourself against any negativity that may chip away at your dream. If your friends or family members insist on attacking it, you may need to place your dream off-limits as a topic of conversation. If they still won't respect your wishes, you may need to spend less time with them.

Your enemies and your friends can be dream killers. But there's one more dream assassin you need to watch out for. And as amazing as it might seem, this last one is even closer to you than the first two.

YOURSELF

Have you ever known someone who was his or her own worst enemy?

At the 1988 Summer Olympics in Seoul, Ben Johnson and Carl Lewis competed in the finals of the hundred-meter dash. They were clearly the two fastest men on the planet, and the one who walked away with the gold medal would be declared the World's Fastest Human. When the gun fired, both men exploded out of the starting blocks, but immediately Johnson began to pull ahead. Lewis, who wasn't accustomed to finishing second, was astonished by Johnson's incredible pace. And it *was* incredible. Johnson's time of 9.79 seconds shattered the previous world record of 9.83.

But that's not the end of the story.

Thirty-six hours after the race, Olympic judges stripped Johnson of his gold medal when a drug test showed large amounts of stanozolol in his system. Stanozolol is a banned anabolic steroid that artificially increases muscle mass and strength and shortens the recovery time between workouts. Ben Johnson is the classic example of a guy whose dream was killed, not by his enemies or his friends, but by himself. He was his own dream assassin.

Could it be that, even as you're reading these words, *you* are your dream's worst enemy? Have you slipped into some bad habits that have become like a ball and chain around your ankle? Have you grown lazy? Are you hanging out with negative people? Are you trying to do too many things at once? Are you compromising your integrity in a way that could bring you shame instead of success?

Recently, the University of Alabama fired its head football coach, Mike Price—before he ever coached a game. His dream had been to stand on the sideline and call the shots for the legendary Crimson Tide. But one ill-advised visit to a strip club tarnished his image to the extent that the university no longer felt comfortable employing him.

One bad decision made in a fleeting moment can be all it takes to destroy a very noble dream.

When Sir Edmund Hillary returned from the summit of Mount Everest, reporters bombarded him with questions about the mind-boggling feat he and his loyal Sherpa, Tenzing Norgay, had accomplished. Question after question focused on their quest to conquer the tallest mountain on earth. Finally, when he could take it no more, he set the record straight. "It was not the mountain we conquered, it was ourselves," he said.

> ONE BAD DECISION MADE IN A FLEETING MOMENT CAN BE ALL IT TAKES TO DESTROY A VERY NOBLE DREAM.

Understand this, my friend: first and foremost, every great dreamer must conquer himself. Friends and enemies alike may throw stumbling blocks in your way, but in the end, you will determine whether your dream lives or dies.

, , ,

Before I close this chapter, let me point out one more important truth. It's simply that God doesn't take kindly to dream killers. Check out Numbers 14:36–38: "Then the ten scouts who had incited the rebellion against the LORD by spreading discouraging reports about the land were struck dead with a plague before the LORD. Of the twelve who had explored the land, only Joshua and Caleb remained alive."

Of course, I'm not suggesting that God is going to strike you or anyone else dead with a plague if you dare to utter a negative word to a dreamer. But clearly, He came down hard on those who tried to kill Caleb and Joshua's dream.

Therefore, when someone shares a dream with you, be cautious in what you say. Even if the dream sounds a little crazy, choose your words carefully. The last thing you want is to have blood on your hands. If a dream is going to die, let it be of natural causes, not murder.

THREE

GETTING GOD
INVOLVED

With God's help we will do mighty things.

—DAVID (PSALM 60:12)

WHEN I FIRST STARTED OUT IN THE MINISTRY,
I was advised by those who were older and more experienced to make sure I treated everybody in my congre-
gation the same. "Don't have favorites," they said,
"because it will create jealousy and resentment." So, for
the first few years, I tried my best not to show any par-
tiality. There were times when I actually socialized with

people who annoyed me and felt guilty for spending time with people I enjoyed.

Finally, I wised up and chucked the whole concept.

If there's one thing I know, it's that I am drawn to some people more than others. It has nothing to do with love. I can honestly say that I love everybody and do my best to prove it in the way that I conduct my ministry. But at the same time, I connect with some people better than others. I understand some people better than others. I admire and respect some people more than others. I have more in common with some people than with others. And yes, I enjoy some people more than others.

So I confess: I have favorites. I've always had favorites, even when I wasn't courageous enough to admit it. And no, I don't feel guilty. Not anymore. Why? Because I finally came to understand a powerful truth: God has favorites too.

Oh yes, He loves everybody. John 3:16 settles that question once and for all. But at the same time, we can see throughout Scripture that God was drawn to certain individuals more than others, and He granted them special privileges and blessings. For example, who would dare to argue that God didn't have special feelings for Noah and his family (Gen. 6:17–18)? Or that He didn't share a special friendship with Abraham (James 2:23)? Or that He didn't put a hedge of protection around Joseph (Gen. 39:2)? Or that He didn't see great potential in an obscure shepherd boy named David (1 Sam. 16:12–13)? Or that He didn't favor Mary over all the young Jewish girls in Judea (Luke 1:26–28)?

And then there's Caleb.

In Numbers 14:24, God made no secret of his special feelings for this high-energy dreamer. He said: "But my servant Caleb is different from the others. He has remained loyal to me, and I will bring him into the land he explored. His descendants will receive their full share of that land."

There's no mistaking the fact that God was a huge Caleb fan, and as such, He was determined to grant him success.

I have no trouble understanding this when I think about how I feel as a fan. For example, I love the St. Louis Cardinals. If I had Godlike power, I would definitely use it to help them win ball games. If needed, I would kick up a little gust of wind to blow a fly ball over the fence.

Or I would make a ground ball take a bad hop to let the winning run score. No, I wouldn't be obvious about it. I wouldn't trip an opposing player on the base paths or cause a pitcher to throw a ball over the backstop.

Okay, so maybe I would.

Let's just say that, in the interest of good taste, I would try to be discreet about my interventions; but I would definitely see to it that my boys came out on top.

And so it is with God.

His special affection for Caleb compelled Him to get involved in Caleb's quest and even to verbally guarantee the fulfillment of his dream. Caleb still had to do his part, and he certainly could have fouled up everything by veering off course. (Remember, this is what happened to Samson!) But as long as he stayed on track, God was going to be in his corner, working on his behalf, helping the pieces fall into place.

The good news is that God hasn't changed, which means that you, too, can win His favor. You, too, can gain Him as an ally in your quest for your dream.

How?

Simply by becoming the kind of person He loves to root for. By becoming the kind of person He loves to bless.

In short, by becoming a person like Caleb.

If you look closely at Numbers 14:24, you'll see that God called attention to three qualities in Caleb. No doubt he possessed other admirable traits, but these are the ones God saw fit to mention as He guaranteed the success of Caleb's dream. Surely, they are the qualities that excite God and make Him want to get involved in our pursuits.

HUMILITY

Notice, first of all, that God called Caleb "my servant." Servants are humble people who recognize their place in the grand scheme of things and do their best to fulfill their obligations to their masters. That God used this word with reference to someone as ambitious as Caleb is quite remarkable. Ambitious people are generally not servants . . . at least, not for very long. Instead, they live with an upward tilt to their chins. They have their eyes on positions of authority. They become the guys who crack the whips and give the orders. So God's use of the word "servant" shows that Caleb managed to strike a delicate balance. It proves that his pursuit of a high and mighty dream never caused him to lose sight of his true position in the grand scheme of things, or his spiritual obligations to his Master.

We know God loved this quality in Caleb, because the Bible speaks again and again of His special affection for humble people. Check out the following verses:

The humble will see their God at work and be glad.
(Ps. 69:32)

Though the LORD is great, he cares for the humble,
but he keeps his distance from the proud.
(Ps. 138:6)

The LORD supports the humble,
but he brings the wicked down into the dust.
(Ps. 147:6)

God sets himself against the proud,
but he shows favor to the humble. (James 4:6)

So humble yourselves under the mighty power of
God, and in his good time he will honor you.
(1 Peter 5:6)

Let me tell you about an incident that brings these verses to life for me.

A few years ago, Poinciana Christian Church was searching for a full-time minister to teens. A number of candidates were considered, but none of them seemed to possess the qualities we were looking for. One day, a young man named Javier Ling called my office and asked if we could have lunch together to discuss the position. I knew of Javier only because another church in the area had recently fired him. I didn't know the whole story, but what I had heard wasn't very flattering. To this day, I can't explain why I agreed to meet with him. Perhaps it was a sense of desperation due to the lack of any outstanding candidates.

Or maybe God was up to something.

We met at a restaurant near Javier's home, and in an odd twist of circumstance, his former boss—the preacher of the church that had just fired him—walked in right after us and took a table across the room. We all nodded and smiled, but the tension level in the room rose significantly. I could tell Javier's emotions were running high. I just knew I was about to hear a sob story about how he had been thoroughly mistreated.

Suddenly, I found myself wishing I had never made the appointment.

But I was wrong.

In what I consider to be one of the greatest displays of humility I've ever witnessed, Javier told me his story. He outlined his mistakes in detail and never once demeaned his former employers. I even asked some questions that gave him every opportunity to bash his former boss, but he never took the bait. I could tell he was bent on being completely honest, even at the risk of costing himself the job.

A few weeks later, we hired Javier. Our leadership team concluded that his past mistakes were more the result of a lack of experience than a flaw in character. We also sensed that he was uniquely gifted for ministry, though he had no track record to substantiate that hunch. In the end, we decided to take a chance. I still tell people that he had the worst credentials of any candidate I've ever interviewed, let alone hired.

But what he did have was a humble, teachable spirit.

Looking back, I'm convinced that God was indeed up to something in that restaurant that day. I believe He was sitting at our table, working on Javier's behalf. I believe He softened my skepticism and opened my heart.

It was a classic James 4:6 moment: God clearly showed favor to a humble young man.

Today, Javier's dreams are coming true in a big way. He's married and has two beautiful children. He's wrapping up his third year with us and has built one of the most dynamic teen ministries in our area. He's proven to be a terrific leader, an excellent counselor, and an effective evangelist. And he's become like a son to me. I shake my head in wonder when I think about all the laws of logic we broke with his hiring.

But that's the point.

The laws of logic mean nothing when God gets involved. His favor can overcome seemingly insurmountable obstacles. And His favor is His gift to those who are humble.

> THE LAWS OF LOGIC MEAN NOTHING WHEN GOD GETS INVOLVED. HIS FAVOR CAN OVERCOME SEEMINGLY INSURMOUNTABLE OBSTACLES.

COURAGE

The second quality that obviously excites God and makes Him want to get involved in the pursuit of our dreams is

43

courage. Again in Numbers 14:24, God said, "My servant Caleb *is different from the others*" (italics mine).

God has always wanted His people to be different.

In the Old Testament, He warned Israel not to intermarry with heathen nations or to adopt their beliefs or their customs (Deut. 7:1–6). In the New Testament, He used Paul's pen to challenge us not to adopt the behavior and customs of the world (Rom. 12:2). And through Peter, He reminded us that He has called us out of the darkness of the world and into God's "wonderful light" (1 Peter 2:9). Some translations even refer to God's children as a "peculiar people."

But it takes great courage to be different in a world that worships conformity.

You'll recall that Joseph was sold into slavery for being different.

Daniel was thrown into a lions' den for being different.

John the Baptist was beheaded for being different.

Jesus was nailed to a cross for being different.

Even Caleb and Joshua were maligned and threatened with stoning because they dared to stand in opposition to the negative report that the other ten spies brought back to Moses.

The reason the world loves conformity is because it breeds a sense of security. It's the age-old idea that if we're all alike, then we're all okay. It's not until one person dares to step out of the crowd and work a little harder or reach a little higher that everybody else looks bad. That's when pressure is applied by the group in an effort to rein in the nonconformist. We call it peer pressure, and it can be very powerful.

A few years ago, a woman I know worked in a corporate office where the boss's birthday was often celebrated with a cake and a stripper. Yes, that's right . . . a cake and a stripper. The employees would gather in the conference room to watch an attractive young woman bump and grind her way around the table to the accompaniment of a portable boom box. There would be hoots and hollers and whistles and cheers, and then everybody would have a piece of cake and go back to work.

It was supposedly all in good fun.

But my friend and one other woman always stayed at their desks and continued working. They didn't preach at the others; they simply made a quiet choice not to participate.

And boy, did they hear about it.

They were said to be party poopers, sticks-in-the-mud, stuck-up, holier-than-thou—you know the drill. And their choice also sparked all sorts of justifications from other employees who claimed to be God-fearing but didn't see anything wrong with a little naughty fun now and then. Their theory, which they intentionally expressed within earshot of the two ladies who bypassed the party, was that people who never loosen up and have some fun give religion a bad name.

The good news is that God fully understands the courage it takes to be different and has promised to bless those, like Caleb, who muster that kind of courage. Read these words very carefully:

> Therefore, come out from them
>> and separate yourselves from them, says the Lord.
> Don't touch their filthy things
>> and I will welcome you.
> *And I will be your Father,*
>> *and you will be my sons and daughters,* says the Lord
>> Almighty. (2 Cor. 6:17–18, italics mine)

I italicized that one line because it is absolutely critical. All loving fathers help their children pursue their dreams, and God has promised to be your Father if you can muster the courage to be different. His favor is His gift to those who dare to step out of the crowd.

LOYALTY

The third quality that excites God and motivates Him to get involved with our dreams is loyalty. In Numbers 14:24, God says, "But my servant Caleb is different from the others. *He has remained loyal to me"* (italics mine).

In that phrase, our eyes are naturally drawn to the word "loyal." But in my view, the word "remained" is just as important. Loyalty comes easy most of the time. For Caleb, marching into the land of Canaan with his "band of brothers" to carry out their spy mission was no test of loyalty at all. But when he saw the giants and the fortified cities . . . when he began

> ALL LOVING FATHERS HELP THEIR CHILDREN PURSUE THEIR DREAMS, AND GOD HAS PROMISED TO BE YOUR FATHER IF YOU CAN MUSTER THE COURAGE TO BE DIFFERENT.

to realize that taking the land wouldn't be as easy as they thought . . . when panic began to spread among his cohorts . . . and when the radical element among the people started talking about stoning him—that's when *remaining* loyal became a real test.

The same thing will happen with you and me.

The vast majority of the time, being loyal to the Lord will be no challenge at all. For example, as I write these words, it is a beautiful spring day. I am sitting in a brand-new office, in a brand-new padded chair, at a brand-new desk, working on an expensive computer that I didn't have to buy. I have slipped my shoes off and am wiggling my toes. I have a chilled bottle of Dasani sitting an arm's length away, and my beautiful wife is in the next room, screening my phone calls. In a little while, I plan to get up and go enjoy a nice lunch, and then come back and write some more.

Life is good.

For the moment.

The thing is, even as I sit here in all this comfort, I know Satan has something up his sleeve. First Peter 5:8 says, "Be careful! Watch out for attacks from the Devil, your great enemy." That verse tells me that he's at the drawing board right this minute, planning a nasty little surprise for me. It might come in the next five minutes, in the form of an irate phone call. Or it might come later this afternoon, in a meeting I'm supposed to attend. I only know that the utopia I'm now enjoying won't last. An attack *is* coming. And when it does, *that's* when my loyalty to the Lord will be put to the test.

The point is that *being* loyal isn't hard.

Remaining loyal is.

Caleb *remained* loyal to the Lord and won God's favor in the process.

, , ,

As I conclude this chapter, I can't help but think about a line I once read about Michael Jordan. I don't remember who wrote it, but it was back in the days when Michael was in his prime, defying gravity, toying with opponents, and winning championships. After a particularly scintillating performance in which he hit an off-balance, last-second shot that lifted his team to victory, one sportswriter wrote, "It's like having God on your team."

The best news I will share with you in this book is this:

You *can* have God on your team.

Not someone *like* God, but God Himself.

He'll suit up and take the court with you. He'll block the shots that would hurt your cause and grab the rebounds you can't reach. He'll pass you the ball and set screens to get you open. And when you're having trouble scoring, He'll stuff one through the hoop Himself. He'll even call time-out when you're winded and need a little rest.

> WHEN GOD IS ON YOUR SIDE, VICTORY BECOMES MORE THAN JUST A POSSIBILITY. YOU SEE, GOD IS UNDEFEATED.

No, He won't do it all for you. You still have to run and jump and sweat and do your part. But He'll be in the game. And, as Caleb discovered, when God is on your side, victory becomes more than just a possibility.

You see, God is undefeated.

FOUR

IN THE FULLNESS OF TIME

The key to everything is patience.
You get the chicken by hatching the egg, not smash-
ing it.

—ARNOLD GLASOW

I WOULD HAVE NO BUSINESS WRITING A BOOK
like this if I didn't have a lifelong dream of my own that
had been fulfilled. I do. In fact, you're holding a piece
of it in your hands. For a long time, my dream has been
to write books about the things of God. But like Caleb,
I had to wait many years to see it happen.

I made my first attempt at writing a book in 1985.

I hammered out the first sixty-five pages of a Christian mystery novel and then asked an English professor to evaluate them for me. When he returned them, virtually every page was marked in red ink, from top to bottom. There were more literary no-no's in those sixty-five pages than in a class full of junior-high term papers. I was embarrassed and destroyed the manuscript.

But I didn't give up my dream.

Instead, I changed my strategy.

Adopting the theory that you have to crawl before you can walk, I decided to try something less ambitious than a novel. A magazine article, it seemed, would be much easier to write and give me a far greater chance of getting published.

Wrong again. Everything I wrote was rejected.

At that point, my confidence was sagging, but I still didn't give up my dream. Instead, I told myself that the time just wasn't right. Maybe I needed more experience. Or more polish as a writer. Or more maturity as a person. Or more and deeper insights into the Word of God and the human condition.

So I let eight years go by and tried again.

This time I wrote a complete book. I didn't dare let

anyone look at it before I finished, for fear that it, too, would get marked up like a junior-high term paper. It took me a year, but I finally banged out the finished product. Then I bought a copy of the *Writer's Market,* put together a proposal exactly according to specifications, and mailed it to twelve publishers.

And promptly got twelve rejections in return.

At that point my ego was wounded and bleeding, but I still didn't give up my dream. Instead, I had a little talk with God. I said, "Okay, Lord, I'm starting to get the idea that this isn't Your will for my life. I'm okay with that, but I just want You to know that it's still something I'd *love* to do. So, if You ever see fit to open the door, I promise I'll give You my best. In the meantime, I'll knuckle down and do the work You've put in front of me."

And I did.

For six more years.

And then, when I least expected it, God began to work.

In the normal flow of life, I met the wonderful Christian novelist Karen Kingsbury. I had read Karen's books and loved them, and I found in her person the same humble, godly spirit that had so drawn me to her stories. Our families became good friends, and though we live three thousand miles apart, we stay in touch and talk often.

One day, as Karen was preparing to fly to Haiti to pick up her adopted sons, I wrote her an e-mail of encouragement. It probably wasn't more than a couple of hundred words. In my mind, it was nothing special, just a word of assurance that some friends and I would be praying for her safety. But somehow, it touched Karen's heart and she wrote back these words:

> Mark . . . that email was so amazing. I even shared it with the kids in our morning devotions. You should be writing your own books. When I get back from this trip, let's talk about it.

I froze.

You should be writing your own books.

I remember staring at the computer screen and blinking my eyes. Surely, I had to be seeing things. No one other than my wife had ever shown any interest in my writing, but suddenly, one of the finest writers in America was telling me I ought to be writing my own books. I had never shared my dream with Karen. I had actually made it a point *not* to mention it because aspiring writers ask her for help all the time, and I didn't want her to think that I was trying to take advantage of our friendship.

I remember praying, *Is this You, God?*

It was.

When Karen returned from Haiti, she insisted that I start writing. She told me to pick a topic I was passionate about and go for it. And she began coaching me. Even with her jam-packed schedule and two more children in the house, she took the time to read my work and critique it. She whittled away a few rough edges (okay, *lots* of rough edges) and made valuable suggestions. And then, when she thought I was ready, she told her agent about me.

Suddenly, doors were opening right and left. Powerful, influential people were taking an interest in my work, and in April 2003, Thomas Nelson published my first book, *The Samson Syndrome.* And now, here you are, holding my second Nelson book in your hands.

It took eighteen years from that first sad attempt at a novel.

Eighteen *long* years.

But here we are: you, me, and God, meeting together in the pages of this book.

Don't ever tell me that dreams don't come true.

But what I learned is this: they don't always come true when *you* want them to.

DIVINE DELAYS

We live in a terribly fast-paced world. We're so used to getting things in a hurry that we go from Dr. Jekyll to Mr. Hyde if we have to wait even a few seconds longer than we think is reasonable. Notice how instantly irritable you get if the guy ahead of you sits a little too long at a red light. Or think about how many times you've rolled your eyes and grumbled under your breath because the checkout girl in the express lane had to run and do a price check. We want our stuff, and we want it now!

> OUR BEST FRIEND IN THE DREAM BUSINESS, GOD HIMSELF, IS OFTEN RESPONSIBLE FOR THE DELAYS WE EXPERIENCE.

But when it comes to our dreams, we simply must

develop a whole new perspective. Worthwhile dreams have many enemies (as I pointed out in chapter 2) and usually encounter many obstacles. In fact, my study of the Scriptures has convinced me that our best friend in the dream business, God Himself, is often responsible for the delays we experience. Let me suggest a few reasons for these divine delays.

First, God may love your dream and its fulfillment might well be on His agenda, but He may have other things He wants to do first. Remember that God is sovereign. He has a plan for this world, and He is going to unfold it as He sees fit, no matter how anxious or restless we may be.

That was certainly the case with Caleb. He was all charged up and ready to go busting into the land of Canaan in Numbers 13. But God slammed the door because He had something else He wanted to take care of first. There were whiners and crybabies that he wanted to weed out of the population. And He decided to do it by sending them on a forty-year trek through the wilderness (Num. 14:29–30). In essence, He was saying to Caleb, "Sorry, My friend. I haven't forgotten you, but I want to take care of this other problem first."

And here's a point you must not miss: that forty-year delay, as difficult as it must have been for Caleb to endure, actually sweetened his dream when it finally did come true. Imagine how frustrated he would have been, trying to battle the sons of Anak with all those whiners and malcontents resisting his every command! But with all of them dead and buried, he was able to assemble a first-rate team that was upbeat and ready for action.

In 2003, the Tampa Bay Buccaneers won the Superbowl in Jon Gruden's first year as coach of that team. I found it interesting to hear him say that his biggest challenge from day one was to get his players to trust him and buy into his plan. As Christians, if we want to be winners we need to trust God and buy into *His* plan. The Bible tells us that He is a God of order and design (1 Cor. 14:33). We need to believe that He knows what He's doing, that He will take first things first and bless our dreams when the time is right. With David, we need to say, "I wait quietly before God, for my hope is in him" (Ps. 62:5).

Second, God may be giving you time to prepare for what your dream come true will require of you. If your dream came true, would it put great demands on your time? If so, maybe God is waiting for you to become more disciplined and organized so that you won't get in over your head.

Would your dream come true require you to spend significant amounts of time away from your spouse or your children? If so, maybe God is giving you time to deepen those relationships so they can stand up to the strain.

Would your dream come true put you in a position of leadership where great numbers of people would look to you for help and guidance? If so, maybe God is giving you time to work on your management and people skills.

Perhaps you've noticed that many great Bible heroes went through a period of preparation before God called them to greatness. Moses, for example, lived in a wilderness for many years before God called him to lead His people through one. Joshua humbly served as Moses' understudy, hungrily devouring the timeless principles of leadership that eventually made him one of the great heroes of the faith. And Jesus patiently taught and trained the disciples for three years before He turned them loose to build His church.

If your dream seems to be on hold, I encourage you to spend some time thinking about the specific ways your life would change if your dream suddenly came true. Then ask yourself if you're ready to handle those changes in a way that would glorify God. This, of course, will require brutal honesty. In fact, you may not be objective enough to perform this type of intense self-examination. Many people aren't. For that reason, I suggest that you ask a trusted (and honest) friend to help you.

The bottom line is this: if there's any hint that you're not physically, mentally, emotionally, or spiritually prepared to handle your dream come true, then get to work. Even as you read these words, God might be waiting for you to do your part before He does His.

Third, God may be waiting for you to show more passion for the little thing He's already given you before He gives you something bigger. I once had a preacher friend who was very likable. He was a funny guy with a cheerful disposition and everybody who knew him enjoyed his company. But he was one of the laziest people I've ever met. He almost never studied. He threw all of his sermons together in an hour or less (usually on Saturday night), pulling them out of whatever sermon book he had on hand. I know this because he talked openly about it. Week after week, he depended on his sense of humor and gift of gab to carry him through, and as a result, his sermons were rambling and tedious.

The odd thing is that he always dreamed of preaching in a large church. He sent out countless resumes and traveled to interviews several states away. On numerous occasions, he was convinced that the church of his dreams was about to hire him, but it never happened. Again and again, he was disappointed.

I once suggested that if he were ever called to a large church, he might have to start spending more time on his sermons. His response was telling. He said, "That would be okay. I wouldn't mind studying ten times as much if I were preaching to ten times as many people."

But according to Jesus, that's not how it works. He said that those who are faithful in little things would be given bigger things (Matt. 25:21, 23, 29). My friend wasn't being faithful in his little church. He wasn't giving his best effort in the ministry God had already given him. Yet, he somehow thought God should reward him.

I don't pretend to know the mind of God, but I have a strong suspicion that if my friend had been a diligent worker, one who strived to reach his potential from day one, God would have blessed him with that so-called "church of his dreams."

Are you like my friend? Are you a slacker who's always gotten by on personality and people skills? Have you relied on your natural talent in the heat of the moment, instead of working hard to develop it?

Boy, that's a tough question, isn't it? But it's one you need to answer if you've been waiting a long time for your dream to come true. I don't know of a single place in the Bible where God rewarded a loafer. On the other hand, Proverbs 13:4 says, "Lazy people want much but get little, but those who work hard will prosper and be satisfied."

> I DON'T KNOW OF A SINGLE PLACE IN THE BIBLE WHERE GOD REWARDED A LOAFER.

Fourth, God may be waiting for you to deal with some sin in your life. If you're a parent, you'll have no problem grasping this idea. You know how easy it is to grant your child's wishes when he's obedient and respectful. But when he sasses you . . . leaves his chores undone . . . or worse yet, when he blatantly disobeys the rules you've set up, you're not receptive at all to his requests. David tells us that it's the same with God. He said, "If I had not confessed the sin in my heart, my Lord would not have listened" (Ps. 66:18).

Right now, sin may be the only thing standing between you and the fulfillment of your dream. You may be smarter and more talented than others who have done what you dream of doing. You may have fully prepared yourself to succeed, and you may have shown passion in the small things God has given you to do. But God may be ignoring your prayers and actively slamming every door of opportunity because of some sinful habit or attitude with which you've grown comfortable. He may be actively opposing you as a way of disciplining you for your disobedience (Heb. 12:6–8).

One time, an old Bible ended up in our lost-and-found box at church. As I thumbed through it, I noticed that the owner had highlighted or underlined every verse he could find that contained a promise of God's blessing. *Very nice,* I thought, until I noticed something odd. In many cases, the person had failed to highlight the conditions that were attached to the promises. For example, Psalm 37:4 says, "Take delight in the LORD, and he will give you your heart's desires." The owner had highlighted the second half of the verse, but not the first!

Question: are you living your life the way that man marked his Bible?

Are you ignoring the conditions of God's promises?

Are you assuming that God will bless you, even if you're not living for Him?

Are you telling yourself that you'll still get the desires of your heart, even if you're not taking delight in Him?

If so, wake up. It doesn't work that way.

Matthew 6:33 says God "will give you all you need from day to day *if you live for him* and make the Kingdom of God your primary concern" (italics mine).

, , ,

What I've realized is that our dreams come true in the fullness of time. They come true when God, in His infinite wisdom, says the time is right. Proverbs 16:9

says, "We can make our plans, but the LORD deter-mines our steps."

Our job is simply to be faithful in the meantime.

In chapter 5 Caleb will show us exactly what that means.

FIVE

YOUR PART IN
THE PROCESS

Don't wait for your ship to come in. Swim out to
meet it.

—MAC ANDERSON

IN 1985 I HAD AN OPPORTUNITY TO MEET
Whitey Herzog, who, at that time, was the manager of
the St. Louis Cardinals. Another preacher and I sat in his
Busch Stadium office for about twenty minutes. We were
there to talk about the team's Sunday morning chapel
services, but Whitey, who is one of the great storytellers
of all time, took off in a dozen different directions. I will

never forget one story he told about Darrell Porter, who was the team's starting catcher and a devout Christian.

The day before our meeting, Darrell had struck out three times with runners on base. The thing that infuriated Whitey was that Darrell never took the bat off of his shoulder. He watched nine consecutive fastballs go by—all belt high and right down the middle—and never swung the bat.

After the game, Whitey called Darrell into his office. "Darrell, what's the problem? You're killing us out there!"

"I don't know, Whitey. I guess when the Lord wants me to hit, I'll hit."

To which Whitey replied, "Darrell, the Lord is a good guy, but He can't help you if you refuse to swing the bat!"

Though no one will ever accuse Whitey Herzog of being a great Bible scholar, that was a pretty nice piece of theology. The Bible teaches that God blesses the *efforts* of His people. Among other places, we can see this truth in the ark that Noah built, in the sling and the stones of a boy named David, and in the missionary journeys of the apostle Paul.

We can also see it in Caleb's quest for his dream.

During those forty-five years that passed between

the birth and the fulfillment of his dream, Caleb was busy doing all the things that would ultimately make his dream come true. In particular, he made five very smart moves. The same ones you must employ if you want to see the fulfillment of your lifelong dream.

SMART MOVE #1

CALEB WORKED AT KEEPING HIS FAITH STRONG

When we meet Caleb at the age of forty, his faith is vibrant and strong. Then, when we meet him again at the age of eighty-five, it's just as strong, or even stronger! What makes this fact so amazing is the environment he was trapped in during those forty-five years. As the following passage shows, he was surrounded by whiny, faithless people.

Then all the people began weeping aloud, and they cried all night. Their voices rose in a great chorus of complaint against Moses and Aaron. "We wish we had died in Egypt, or even here in the wilderness," they wailed. "Why is the LORD taking us to this country

69

only to have us die in battle? Our wives and little ones will be carried off as slaves! Let's get out of here and return to Egypt!" (Num. 14:1–3)

Clearly, Caleb wasn't just trapped in a physical desert. He was also trapped in a spiritual desert! The only way he could have survived the relentless bellyaching of his countrymen was to connect with God and stay connected.

> LIKE CALEB, YOU'RE PROBABLY GOING TO HAVE TO TREK THROUGH A FEW DESERTS ON THE WAY TO YOUR DREAM. AND YOU MAY HAVE TO DO IT IN THE COMPANY OF SOME WHINY, FAITHLESS PEOPLE.

It's no different with you. Like Caleb, you're probably going to have to trek through a few deserts on the way to your dream. And you may have to do it in the company of some whiny, faithless people. So, right now, you might as well come to grips with a powerful truth that is the foundation upon which all of your hopes and dreams will always rest: the likelihood of your lifelong dream coming true will correspond directly to the strength of your faith.

Why? Because faith has always been the thing that moves God to action on our behalf. Jesus said, "Anything is possible if a person believes" (Mark 9:23), and "If you believe, you will receive whatever you ask for in prayer" (Matt. 21:22).

One day while I was preaching, I held up a sign and asked my people to read it. The sign said:

GODISNOWHERE

Immediately, several people blurted out, "God is nowhere!" Then, two or three seconds after that initial response, somebody cried, "No! It says, God is *now here!*" The illustration worked just as I'd hoped and gave me a wonderful teaching opportunity. I'm sorry to say that, for a lot of people, the first response to any problem is to say, "God is nowhere! God has abandoned me!" That's the very thing we must avoid. To experience God's power in our lives . . . to have our prayers answered . . . to see our dreams come true, we've got to maintain a "God is now here" mentality.

People have written many wonderful books about

growing and maintaining a strong faith. A host of knowledgeable Christians have offered worthwhile suggestions. Let me just say that, in my experience, the single most important thing you can do to maintain a "God is now here" frame of mind is stay in the Word of God.

A few years ago, a wonderful young woman in our church was diagnosed with terminal pancreatic cancer. That's always a tough situation, but in her case, it felt especially heartbreaking because she'd been married for only a few years and had a beautiful young daughter. I was sitting with her family when the doctor gave them the grim news: she had two years or less to live, and she would experience a lot of pain as the cancer progressed.

A couple of days later, I walked into her hospital room and found her all alone. Her family had gone to lunch, so it was just the two of us. She said, "I'm glad they're gone. I've been wanting to talk to you."

"What's on your mind?" I asked.

She looked serious. "I want you to tell me if I'm crazy."

I was puzzled. "What makes you think you might be crazy?"

"Well," she said, "forty-eight hours ago, my doctor told me I'm going to die in less than two years. Everybody I know is completely torn up about it. There've been enough tears shed in this room to float a battleship—but none of them have been mine."

And then she reached down and picked up her Bible. "I've been reading this," she said, "and the more I read it, the better I feel about everything. I know I'm supposed to be really upset. My family keeps telling me I'm in denial, and that one of these days I'm going to crash. But I don't think so. The more I read this, the more I just feel like everything's going to be okay . . . one way or the other."

I had to smile. It was one of the most beautiful testimonies I'd ever heard. What she was experiencing was the promise of Romans 10:17: "Faith comes from listening to this message of good news." The horrible circumstances of her life weren't destroying her because the Word of God was overpowering them. The good news was enriching her faith, so that even as her body grew weaker, her trust in the Lord was growing stronger.

I said, "My dear, you're not the least bit crazy. You've just discovered one of the greatest secrets of dynamic Christian living: the Word of God builds our faith and keeps it strong, no matter what's going on around us."

Dear reader, you may never be diagnosed with terminal cancer, but plenty of other challenges will threaten your faith, and therefore your dream. Job 5:7 says, "People are born for trouble as predictably as sparks fly upward from a fire." As you wait for your dream to come true—whether it takes a week, a year, or fifty years—you need to constantly feed on God's Word. Read it, study it, and listen to it preached. The psalmist said, "Your principles have been the music of my life throughout the years of my pilgrimage" (Ps. 119:54).

Caleb didn't write those words, but he could have. He obviously worked at keeping his faith strong.

SMART MOVE #2

CALEB GOT OTHER PEOPLE EXCITED ABOUT HIS DREAM

When we come to Joshua 14, the wilderness years are past, the Israelites have finally crossed into the land of Canaan, and the time has come to divide the remaining unconquered land among the various tribes. Verse 6 is easy to overlook, but it's significant. It says, "A delegation from the tribe of Judah, led by Caleb son of Jephunneh the Kenizzite, came to Joshua at Gilgal."

The first thing that strikes me here is that Caleb was respectful of authority. There's an old saying that it's always easier to get forgiveness than permission, so go ahead and do what you want and deal with the consequences later. But Caleb didn't operate that way. The thought of charging off into the hills of Hebron without Joshua's approval never occurred to him. And if Joshua had refused to grant his request, I have no doubt that Caleb would have respected his decision. In our world, where there is so much outright contempt for authority, Caleb's submissive spirit feels as refreshing as an autumn breeze. And it surely is one of the reasons God so richly blessed him.

But notice that Caleb wasn't alone when he went to ask for permission to conquer the hill country of Hebron. He showed up with a delegation: a group of men who were standing behind him, showing their support for his dream and their willingness to help him achieve it. Apparently, Caleb had been talking to these men about his dream, and now they were catching his vision. *His* dream had become *their* dream!

75

What about *your* dream? Have you shared it with anyone?

Or have you been reluctant to talk about it because you're afraid that others might think it's silly?

Let's face it. If anybody ever had a "silly" dream, it was Caleb. Remember, he was eighty-five years old when he set out to conquer the hill country of Hebron. Most guys his age were sitting in rocking chairs with afghans over their laps!

IF YOUR DREAM SEEMS SILLY TO SOME, CONGRATULATIONS! YOU'RE IN EXCELLENT COMPANY!

Also, consider this: *every* truly great dream is a silly dream. Imagine the belly laughs that must have rung out the first time somebody talked about men being able to fly. And what about Walt Disney? The entertainment empire that bears his name is second to none today, but he had a terrible time getting started because people just weren't enthused about his little cartoon mouse. So if your dream seems silly to some, congratulations! You're in excellent company!

I encourage you to do what Caleb did. Talk about your dream. Not with everybody, because some people will just ridicule you and tear it down. (Remember those dream killers we talked about earlier?) But share it with people you trust and who love you. Share it with people who are known visionaries. Share it with people who've seen their own dreams come true. Just talking about it will help you sharpen and more clearly define it. And who knows? Someday you just might find what Caleb found: a whole bunch of people lined up behind you who are willing to help you make it happen.

Smart Move #3

CALEB KEPT HIMSELF IN GOOD PHYSICAL CONDITION

In Joshua 14:10–11, Caleb said to Joshua, "Today I am eighty-five years old. I am as strong now as I was when Moses sent me on that journey, and I can still travel and fight as well as I could then."

Do you realize how amazing that statement is?

As I write these words, I am forty-seven, and while I am not a pathetic slob by any means, I am forced to admit that I am not as strong as I was even ten years ago. When our Monday night church softball games are

77

over, I am whipped. In fact, each new season seems to bring a whole new set of aches and pains. I am to the point now where it takes me longer to put on my tape and knee braces than it does to play the game. And, in what is perhaps the most telling indication of the changes happening in my body, we are now buying the ten-gallon-bucket size of Advil.

But I keep playing ball, because I wouldn't want to deprive my teammates of the privilege of heckling me. When one of my bloopers finds a hole and I manage to pull into second with a double, I rather enjoy the calls for oxygen and a stretcher that always come flying out of our dugout. "Old Man River," they call me. He just keeps rolling along. Or hobbling, to be more accurate.

That's why I have so much respect for Caleb. In a generation when there were no multivitamins or Soloflex machines . . . at a time when he couldn't pop a tape into the VCR and "sweat to the oldies" with Richard Simmons, the man was able to maintain his health and strength into his mid-eighties!

I once heard it said that you can tell how healthy a person is by watching what he takes two at a time: stairs or pills. Unfortunately, most Americans are taking fistfuls of pills and riding elevators. It's been reported in numerous publications that Americans are by far the fattest people on earth, and I believe it. The next time you're at a shopping mall or a ball game, just look around. Obesity is everywhere, even in young children. And if obesity is everywhere, you know lots of other physical problems are too. In fact, obesity is now considered the number-one health problem in America because so many other health problems spin off of it.

Wouldn't it be awful if you carried a dream in your heart for forty years and finally got a chance to make it come true, only to have health problems shut you out? Of course, we have no control over some health problems. But studies have shown that we can greatly reduce the risk of most illnesses by eating right, exercising, and lowering stress.

WOULDN'T IT BE AWFUL IF YOU CARRIED A DREAM IN YOUR HEART FOR FORTY YEARS AND FINALLY GOT A CHANCE TO MAKE IT COME TRUE, ONLY TO HAVE HEALTH PROBLEMS SHUT YOU OUT?

If you're serious about your dream, you need to think about your health habits. And you need to see a doctor regularly. I am continually astonished at the number of people who haven't had a physical in years. Are you one of them? If you are, you're just asking for something bad to happen. Something that could mean the end of your lifelong dream.

Smart Move #4

CALEB ASKED FOR HIS DREAM

I touched on this earlier, but I want to hit it again from a different angle. Caleb marched right up to his friend, Joshua, who was in charge of the distribution of the land, and put in his official request: "I'm asking you to give me the hill country that the LORD promised me" (Josh. 14:12).

When I read that verse, a New Testament Scripture immediately comes to mind: "The reason you don't have what you want is that you don't ask God for it" (James 4:2). If we were as bold in our prayer lives as Caleb was before Joshua, I suspect we'd see a lot more of our dreams coming true.

Praying people have always moved God. In fact, praying people have actually been known to change

God's mind! Remember when God was all set to destroy Sodom and Gomorrah—until Abraham interceded? He pleaded with God to spare the city if only ten righteous people could be found within it . . . and God agreed (Gen. 18:20–33).

Or what about the time God's anger burned hot against the faithless Israelites? In His fury, He said He would wipe them out and start all over, but Moses interceded on their behalf and God relented (Num. 14:11–20).

Or what about the beautiful parable Jesus told about the home owner who was awakened in the middle of the night by a knock at his door? He called out, "Don't bother me!" and turned over to go back to sleep. But because the person at the door kept knocking, the home owner finally got up and answered (Luke 11:5–8). Jesus followed up that parable with these words: "And so I tell you, keep on asking, and you will be given what you ask for. Keep on looking, and you will find. Keep on knocking, and the door will be opened. For everyone who asks, receives. Everyone who seeks, finds. And the door is opened to everyone who knocks" (Luke 11:9–10).

If you're carrying a big dream in your heart and if you believe in the truthfulness of God's Word, then those words must send shivers down your spine. Their implications are staggering!

Let me tell you about a woman I met several years ago who dared to claim the promise of Luke 11:9–10.

Her name was Cynthia, and her husband had abandoned her. She knew that he had taken up with a woman half his age and moved to a town one hundred miles away. She knew that they were indulging their romantic fantasies, parading around the community as if they were husband and wife, and even attending church together. Friends encouraged Cynthia to badger her husband: ruffle his little love nest and make his life miserable. But she refused.

She chose, instead, to pray.

Every morning, when she sat down at the kitchen table to have her coffee, she set out two cups, two spoons, and two napkins. "Lord," she prayed, "let this be the day he comes walking through that door and sits down to have coffee with me."

But day after day, month after month, and year after year, when she got up to clear the table, she put his cup away unused.

Still, Cynthia believed the promise of Luke 11:9–10.

She believed the key was to *keep* asking, *keep* looking, and *keep* knocking. She once said to me, "It doesn't bother me that God hasn't yet answered my prayer. I know he loves my husband even more than I do, and I believe this very minute He's working on my husband in ways I can't even imagine. I'm willing to trust Him. I believe something great is going to happen."

One morning—after more than two years of living alone—Cynthia sat at her kitchen table with two cups and two spoons in front of her. Suddenly, she heard a car pull into the driveway. Her heart beat faster, but she didn't get up to look out the window. She simply glanced at his empty cup, and then toward the ceiling. "Is it him, Father?"

Seconds later, she heard a key slip into the locked kitchen door and turn the bolt. The door swung open, and her husband stepped into the room. With tears in her eyes, Cynthia smiled and said, "I've been expecting you."

When I share that story with Christians, I get a wide range of reactions. Some people are moved to tears and encouraged in their faith. But others become cynical. Some have even said, "That's fairy-tale stuff. Things like that don't happen in real life!"

My question is simply this: is Luke 11:9–10 true, or isn't it?

If it is, then Cynthia's story, which really happened, isn't hard to believe at all.

Remember, we have a God who is able to do "infinitely more than we would ever dare to ask or hope" (Eph. 3:20).

It boils down to this: the people who label Cynthia's story a fantasy and close their minds to such awesome possibilities will almost certainly fail to see their lifelong dreams come true. But the people who believe in their hearts that God is not only capable, but also delights in doing such things, are well on their way.

Which type of person are you?

SMART MOVE #5

CALEB COMMITTED TO FIGHT THE TOUGH BATTLES

Caleb was never under any illusions about what his dream would require in terms of sweat and sacrifice. When he stood before Joshua, he said, "You will remember that as scouts we found the Anakites living there in great, walled cities. But if the LORD is with me, I will drive them out of the land, just as the LORD said" (Josh. 14:12).

Caleb could have sent his men out to do the dirty work. He could have pulled an Osama bin Laden and retreated to a cave to orchestrate the campaign from a safe distance. But he seemed to understand that for his dream to come true—for it to have any real meaning— he would have to get his hands dirty.

I know a young man who started a restaurant when he was in his twenties. He scraped together the money and opened a little Italian café near his home. Even though he was the boss, he was the first one to work in the morning and the last one to leave in the evening. He did the purchasing, the cooking, and even waited tables and mopped floors. Over the years, the business grew and relocated to a larger building. It was a huge success.

Then one day, a man walked in and offered to buy the business. The offer was well up into the six figures, many times the amount of the owner's initial investment. So he sold out. He socked the huge profit in the bank and immediately began preparing to start all over with a new business.

Can you guess what happened to the little Italian café? It went broke and was closed in less than two years.

Why? Because the new owner wasn't willing to fight the tough battles. He wanted the profits, but he wasn't willing to put in the long hours and make the hard sacrifices that the original owner had made. He wanted to let other people do the work while he sat back and counted the money.

> TO SEE THE FULFILLMENT OF YOUR LIFELONG DREAM, YOU'VE GOT TO BE MORE THAN JUST A DREAMER. YOU'VE ALSO GOT TO BE A DOER. YOU'VE GOT TO BE WILLING TO FIGHT THE TOUGH BATTLES.

Think about the most successful people you know; the people who have fulfilled their lifelong dreams. Take a moment and picture a few of them in your mind. I'm guessing that there's not a lazy person in the bunch. I'm guessing that they're all scrappy and tenacious. I'm guessing that they've all got a few battle scars they could show you.

You think that's a coincidence?

No way. To see the fulfillment of your lifelong dream, you've got to be more than just a dreamer. You've also got to be a doer. You've got to be willing to fight the tough battles.

Robert Townsend is the author of the best-selling book *Up the Organization*, and has been one of the most respected businessmen in America for the last fifty years. His leadership success with American Express and Avis have made him a man that dreamers everywhere want to listen to. But people are often surprised when they find out what Robert Townsend believes.

He believes that nobody should have a special parking place.

Nobody should have special stationery.

There should be no company plane.

There should be no free country-club memberships.

And he believes that leaders should never delegate grunt work. In fact, even at the peak of his career, he refused to have a secretary and always answered his own phone.

The question is, why?

Simply because he believed that humble people, who are willing to work hard in pursuit of their dreams, stand the best chance of seeing them come true.[2]

After studying the life of Caleb, I find that philosophy hard to argue with. Caleb was a man of great faith, to be

sure. But he never took a shortcut and was always willing to pull more than his share of the load. Of course,
some people will maintain that guys like Caleb are just
lucky. But do you believe that?

, , ,

Right now, the time has come for you to decide just
how committed you are to your dream. If it truly is the
passion of your heart, then I challenge you:

To keep your faith strong,

To share your dream with others,

To take care of your health,

To pray hard,

And to fight all the tough battles.

There are no shortcuts to a dream come true.

SIX

WHAT TO DO WHEN YOUR DREAM COMES TRUE

We do not respect men for their riches, but for their philanthropy; just as we do not value the sun for its height, but for its warmth.

—GAMALIEL BAILEY

IF YOU ASK PEOPLE IF THEY'VE HEARD OF Matthew Webb, you'll get a lot of head scratching and eyebrow scrunching. But there was a time when Matthew Webb was a household name. You could even make the case that he was, for a short time, the most famous man in the world.

It was early in the afternoon on August 24, 1875,

that the twenty-seven-year-old Webb jumped off of Admiralty Pier and began what would be the first successful attempt to swim the English Channel. It took him twenty-one hours and forty-five minutes to accomplish the swimmer's equivalent of climbing Mount Everest. He nourished himself along the way with eggs and bacon, coffee, beer, brandy, and cod-liver oil. For almost a full day, he beat the water with an awkward breast stroke and somehow managed to endure the physical torture and stave off the even more frightening mental demons.

When he finally stumbled ashore, he was exhausted, freezing, and half out of his mind . . . but he was victorious. And suddenly famous. He had accomplished what all the experts said was impossible. Accolades poured in from around the world. A French newspaper said that he must be "half man and half fish." In less than twenty-four hours, he had transitioned from obscurity to celebrity, and he did it by fulfilling his lifelong dream.

Yet, Matthew Webb stands out in history as a tragic figure rather than a hero. His life began falling apart within months after his dream came true. He became addicted to the limelight and tried everything he could think of to keep his celebrity status from slipping away. As time passed and this became more and more difficult, he resorted to humiliating stunts. At one point, he even tried to build a career as a motivational speaker. But his communication skills were horrendous and his story was too well known to hold much interest for audiences.

Finally, in what could only be called an act of desperation, Matthew Webb decided to try to regain his popularity by doing something even more outrageous than swimming the English Channel. At the age of thirty-four, and with a wife and two children, he announced that he would travel to America and challenge Niagara Falls in nothing but a bathing suit. His family and friends pleaded with him not to do it, but he turned a deaf ear. He knew his chances of survival were practically nonexistent, but he was desperate to regain his lost glory. Failing that, he was more than happy to die. He simply didn't want to go on living without the ring of applause in his ears.

The history books say that the crushing waters of Niagara Falls killed Matthew Webb, but those who were close to him knew better. He was, in fact, destroyed by success.

Success is so glorified and coveted in our culture that we don't often stop to realize how dangerous it can be. It can inflate your ego, impair your judgment, and disconnect you from your core values. It can place great demands on your time, put pressure on your relationships, and leave you with fewer opportunities to worship your Maker and cultivate your inner strengths. And it can bring dangerous new people into your life: leeches and opportunists who do not have your best interests at heart.

> OUR CULTURE SO GLORIFIES AND COVETS SUCCESS THAT WE DON'T OFTEN STOP TO REALIZE HOW DANGEROUS IT CAN BE.

That's why I can't end this book without talking about what to do when your dream comes true. The greatest tragedy of all would be for you to see the fulfillment of your dream, and then have it ruin you.

AN UNFORGETTABLE GIFT

My favorite part of Caleb's story is the part most people never notice. Most think his story ends as Joshua 14 comes to a close. But Caleb resurfaces briefly in the next chapter, just long enough for us to see him do something amazing.

He'd given his daughter, Acsah, to Othniel, who was one of his finest soldiers. As a wedding present, he gave them a section of the land he'd just conquered, which is something we'd expect from any loving father. It's what he did next that is truly stunning:

> When Acsah married Othniel, she urged him to ask her father for an additional field. As she got down off her donkey, Caleb asked her, "What is it? What can I do for you?" She said, "Give me a further blessing. You have been kind enough to give me the land in the Negev; please give me springs as well." So Caleb gave her the upper and lower springs. (Josh. 15:18–19)

To appreciate those verses, you must understand that the springs represented the most fertile areas. They were the prime real estate, the most valuable section of the territory that Caleb had risked his life to acquire. They were the very heart of his original dream. It was their beauty that had set his heart on fire as a young man and consumed his thoughts for almost a half century.

And without batting an eye, he gave them away.

Not just the upper *or* the lower springs, but the upper *and* the lower!

Granted, there's something almost magical about a father's love for his daughter. I can tell you from personal experience that when Daddy's Little Girl asks for something, there's a good chance she's going to get it. (And, by the way, most of the daddy's girls I know understand this and take full advantage of it!)

THIS ACT OF GENEROSITY ON CALEB'S PART IS TRULY AMAZING. IMAGINE WAITING ALL THOSE YEARS AND RISKING YOUR LIFE TO GET SOMETHING, AND THEN TURNING AROUND AND GIVING IT AWAY!

But be that as it may. Even figuring a father's love into the equation, this act of generosity on Caleb's part is truly amazing. Imagine waiting all those years and risking your life to get something, and then turning around and giving it away!

AN UNMISTAKABLE LESSON

You know, it occurs to me that this part of the story could easily have been left out of the Bible. There's little drama in it. No one's life was in danger. No enemies were threatening our boy, Caleb. God could have omitted it, and we wouldn't have felt a bit shortchanged.

But He didn't.

God saw to it that this bit of information made it into the biblical record, and I can think of only one reason why. I believe He wanted to show us what to do when our dreams come true. He understood the dangers of success and wanted to give us a clear example to follow.

Many people who see their dreams come true face a strong temptation to hang on tight and never let go. After working a lifetime to achieve a great dream, a kind of hoarding mentality can set in. Jesus pictured it for us in one of His most famous parables:

A rich man had a fertile farm that produced fine crops. In fact, his barns were full to overflowing. So he said, "I know! I'll tear down my barns and build bigger ones. Then I'll have enough room to store everything. And I'll sit back and say to myself, 'My friend, you have enough stored away for years to come. Now take it easy! Eat, drink, and be merry!'" But God said to him, "You fool! You will die this very night. Then who will get it all?" (Luke 12:16–20)

Caleb and the rich fool are two guys whose dreams came true. But in every other way, they were as different as night and day. The rich fool represents all the tight-fisted, selfish people who scream, "This is mine! I earned it, and *you* can't have it!" Caleb represents all the big-hearted, generous people who understand that everything belongs to God, even the fruit of their dreams.

Maybe you've heard of Charles Feeney. He's a New Jersey businessman who made a lot of money in duty-free airport shops. Most observers believed he was worth billions, and he was at one time. What they didn't know was that, after his five children were grown, Mr. Feeney started giving his money away. He began funding humanitarian projects in underdeveloped countries and giving grants to hospitals and universities here in the States. Once he even donated $30 million to a single charity! And he did it quietly, taking great pains to protect his identity. It was only during the processing of a legal matter that the public heard of his generosity.

Charles Feeney is a modern-day Caleb in two ways: his lifelong dream came true, and he turned around and gave a big chunk of it away. And if what the Bible says is true—that it's more blessed to give than to receive—then he was twice blessed, and his second blessing was greater than his first.

, , ,

My dreaming friend, as you close this book and lay it down, I pray that you'll take up the Caleb Quest, and that someday, at the time of God's choosing, you'll see the fulfillment of your lifelong dream. But just as fervently, I pray that when it happens, you'll use it to bless others. If you do, I predict you'll make a startling discovery: that the giving away of your dream will bring you more joy than its fulfillment ever did.

DISCUSSION
QUESTIONS

For Personal Reflection or Group Discussion

CHAPTER 1: ASSESSING YOUR DREAM

1. If you have an unfulfilled dream, describe it. Did you find it, or did it find you? Either way, explain how it happened.

2. Does your dream fit with God's will? What specific Scriptures can you point to that confirm this?

3. Does your dream fit with your talents? Specifically, what talents do you possess that you believe are in

harmony with your dream? (Because we sometimes give ourselves more credit than we deserve, I suggest that you ask at least three people who know you well to answer this question.)

4. If your dream came true, how would it affect the people in your world? Specifically, how might it bless them? Can you think of any ways your fulfilled dream might harm or hinder them?

CHAPTER 2: DREAM KILLERS

1. The natural enemies of your dream are the people who stand to suffer if your dream comes true. Who are they? What could they do to make your dream difficult to fulfill? How do you plan to combat their efforts?

2. What kind of support do you get from your family and friends? Can you name a friend or relative who is likely to discourage you as you pursue your dream? What do you believe this person's motivation is? How will you handle this individual and still maintain a positive relationship?

3. What specific mistakes would mean the death of your dream? What safeguards have you built into your life to keep from committing those errors? Do you have an accountability partner who can help you avoid trouble? If not, who could work with you in that capacity?

CHAPTER 3: GETTING GOD INVOLVED

1. God called Caleb "my servant." Could He call you His servant? In what ways are you serving the Lord? How long have you been doing so? Has your service been hit-and-miss or consistent during that time?

2. One of Caleb's finest moments occurred when he stood with Joshua against the other ten spies. Can you give an example of a time when you chose to separate yourself from the majority and suffered as a result? Can you name any blessings that came your way as a result of that choice? Would you make the same choice again?

3. Satan designs his attacks to test our loyalty. Are there specific times, places, or people that Satan uses to draw you away from God? How can you resist those influences?

DISCUSSION QUESTIONS

CHAPTER 4: IN THE FULLNESS OF TIME

1. Have you ever had a dream come true? Describe it. How long did it take? Looking back, could you have done anything to speed up the process?

2. Can you think of a reason why God might be waiting to bless your current dream? Do you need some additional education or experience? Do you need to be attentive to the work God has already given you?

3. Have you ignored a sin in your life? Why haven't you dealt with it? What could you do today to start bringing that sin under control?

CHAPTER 5: YOUR PART IN THE PROCESS

1. Name some things you are doing now specifically to keep your faith strong. Do you find that the strength of your faith fluctuates a lot? What can you do to avoid downtimes?

2. Have you shared your dream with anyone? If not, why? Does something about your dream embarrass

you? Can you think of a person who would be excited to know about your dream and encourage you?

3. Do you have any bad health habits? What are they? Why haven't you corrected them? What changes could you make today that would help you live a longer, healthier life?

4. Do you have a healthy prayer life? Have you ever asked God for your dream? If not, why? Do you feel guilty when you ask God to fulfill your dreams? Why do you think Caleb didn't feel guilty asking Joshua for the hill country of Hebron?

5. Think of someone who is already living the dream you hold in your heart. What battles did that person have to fight? Do you see any of those same battles looming before you? Are you willing to fight them?

CHAPTER 6: WHAT TO DO WHEN YOUR DREAM COMES TRUE

1. Can you name someone you believe success destroyed? Explain why you believe this.

2. What kind of giver are you? Can you name something you gave away that others thought was foolishly extravagant? If so, why did you give it? Would you do it again if you had the chance?

3. If your dream came true, do you think you could turn around and give the biggest portion of it away? If so, whom might you give it to? Why?

ACKNOWLEDGMENTS

JESSAMYN WEST SAID, "WRITING IS A SOLITARY occupation. Family, friends, and society are the natural enemies of the writer. He must be alone, uninterrupted, and slightly savage if he is to sustain and complete an undertaking." These words explain why authors take pains to include an acknowledgments section in their books. After being "slightly savage" for months, we feel compelled to thank the people we love for putting up with us. This time, my gratitude goes out to the following precious souls:

My wife, Marilyn, and my daughter, Michelle. Thanks for making our home an oasis. I wish all families could be as happy as ours.

ACKNOWLEDGMENTS

My parents, Doug and Barbara Atteberry. Thank you for always encouraging me to chase my dreams and for supporting me every step of the way.

My agent, Lee Hough. Thank you for representing me with integrity and class. If we really are known by the company we keep, then you make me look very good.

My editor, Brian Hampton. Mark Twain said, "When you catch an adjective, kill it. No, I don't mean all of them, but kill most of them. Then the rest will be valuable." Thanks, Brian, for pointing out which of my adjectives needed to die.

My friend Kyle Olund, and the Thomas Nelson team. You guys set the standard for professionalism and still manage to make the process fun.

My friend Karen Kingsbury. Thank you for the beautiful foreword and for your continued support and encouragement.

My flock, the members and friends of Poinciana Christian Church. The dream we share for our community is a big one. Thank you for chasing it with me.

NOTES

1. Pam Grout, *Living Big* (New York: MJF Books, 2001) 126–8.
2. Peter Krass, *The Little Book of Business Wisdom: Rules of Success from More Than 50 Business Legends* (Hoboken, N.J.: John Wiley & Sons, Inc., 2000), 34–37.

ABOUT THE AUTHOR

MARK ATTEBERRY, a graduate of St. Louis Christian College, has been preaching for twenty-eight years and has been the minister of Poinciana Christian Church in Kissimmee, Florida, since 1989. He has spoken and led workshops at the North American Christian Convention and the Florida Christian Convention, as well as at countless camps, colleges, retreats, and revivals. Mark is also an accomplished jazz saxophonist, an avid collector of fine jazz recordings, and a sports fan. He has been married for twenty-eight years to his high-school sweetheart, Marilyn. They have one daughter, Michelle.

For more information on Mark, visit:
www.MarkAtteberry.net

NEW FROM MARK ATTEBERRY!

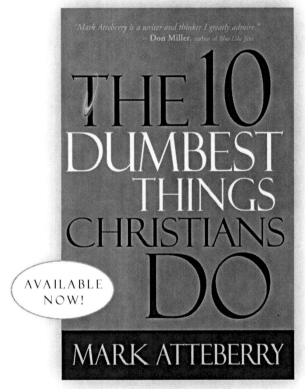

"Mark Atteberry is a writer and thinker I greatly admire."
— Don Miller, author of Blue Like Jazz

THE 10 DUMBEST THINGS CHRISTIANS DO

AVAILABLE NOW!

MARK ATTEBERRY

PASTOR MARK ATTEBERRY inspires and equips Christians to take a fresh look at why their efforts to serve God are often woefully ineffective. Atteberry outlines the unintentionally dumb things that explain why the world has a hard time taking Christians seriously, and how they provide Satan with a never-ending supply of opportunities to make the people of God look foolish.

ISBN: 0-7852-1148-9 | $13.99

Visit ThomasNelson.com

THOMAS NELSON
Since 1798

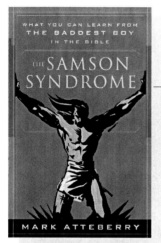

ISBN 0-7852-6447-7

PRAISE FOR
THE SAMSON SYNDROME

"I could not put this book down. Every page was riveting. Why? Because I saw myself on every page. And you will too. This book will change your life."

—PAT WILLIAMS
Senior Vice President of the
Orlando Magic and Author of
How to Be Like Mike and *Unsinkable*

"Mark Atteberry helps us see the Samson in ourselves . . . and take conscious steps to become the men Christ wants us to be."

—RANDY ALCORN
Author of *Safely Home* and *The Treasure Principle*

"Mark Atteberry is the next Max Lucado!"

—KAREN KINGSBURY
Bestselling Author of *Halfway to Forever*
and *A Time to Dance*

"Mark Atteberry very clearly helps us realize the downside of our strengths. My prayer for each reader is that we will be big enough to admit our mistakes, smart enough to profit from them, and strong enough to correct them."

—JOHN C. MAXWELL
Founder of The INJOY Group and
New York Times Bestselling Author

Also from MARK ATTEBERRY...

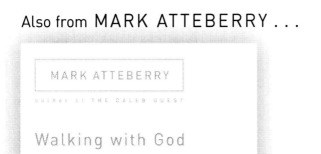

MARK ATTEBERRY

Walking with God

on the Road You Never

Wanted to Travel

available now!

The Christian life isn't always a walk in the park. Taking fourteen strategies from the Israelite journey, Mark Atteberry offers real hope to those on an unexpected, difficult journey. The lessons presented in *Walking with God on the Road You Never Wanted to Travel* are simply stated, clearly explained, and beautifully illustrated with stories of others emerging from unimaginable circumstances.

ISBN: 0-7852-1132-2 | $13.99

Visit ThomasNelson.com

Thomas Nelson
Since 1798

LaVergne, TN USA
11 September 2009
157602LV00004B/8/P